Author: Dr. Michelle Stevens-Oldham
Columbia, SC 29229
drstevensm@gmail.com

BEAUTY OF THE BLACK SWAN
BY
DR. MICHELLE STEVENS-OLDHAM

ALSO BY DR. MICHELLE STEVENS-OLDHAM

High Heels and LipStick

31 Day Journal and Note taker for Women

A book of Inspiration to Healing and Wholeness

From Past Hurt and Pain

BootStraps and BowTies

31 Day Journal and Note Taker for Men

A Book of Inspiration for Men

You are Called and Designed To BE a KING

DR. MICHELLE STEVENS-OLDHAM

BEAUTY OF THE BLACK SWAN

Beauty of the Black Swan is a soulful work of art that embodies **love, perfection, grace**, and the divine essence of a **marvelous woman**. This poetic collection is more than just words on a page—it is a reflection of the journey Black women take from pain to power, from silence to self-expression, and from survival to sacred wholeness. With each verse, the author weaves together strength and vulnerability, resilience and softness, creating a mirror in which women can see their true selves—flawed yet flawless, wounded yet worthy, broken yet beautifully whole.

This book celebrates the intricate layers of womanhood—the spiritual, the sensual, the emotional, and the eternal. It honors the strength it takes to rise, the love it takes to heal, and the grace it takes to keep moving forward. *Beauty of the Black Swan* is a love letter to the Black woman's soul—a call to reclaim her voice, her beauty, and her God-ordained place in the world. Whether you are standing in the ashes or already soaring, these poems will speak to the queen within and remind you that you are, and always have been, enough.

This book may be purchased for educational, business, or promotional use. For information regarding bulk purchases, custom editions, or special orders, please get in touch with the publisher directly.

Printed and published in the United States of America.
This publication is an imprint of **M.S. Oldham Enterprise**.

For permissions, inquiries, or licensing requests, please contact:
forus@directionatmidlife.us

ISBN: 9798218993955
First Edition

Acknowledgments & Gratitude

To my Boo, my wonderful husband, **Rodney Oldham,** thank you for being my rock through every chapter of this journey. You listened to every poem I read aloud, offering your support even when some poems may not have been your favorite. Your patience, your quiet strength, and your unwavering love reflect the very **patience of God**. As I navigated the emotional depths of this project, supported my daughter, your stepdaughter, through her breast cancer battle, and launched my podcast, you stood beside me, never wavering. Your presence was a shelter, your encouragement a constant reminder that I was never walking alone. I am forever grateful.

To the powerful, beautiful women who contributed their voices and hearts to the interludes, thank you. Your love, belief, and authenticity breathe life into this book. Each of you helped shape the rhythm of this work with your vulnerability, your stories, and your sisterhood.

And to my daughter, my heart, thank you for always being my **cheerleader, my teammate, and my safe place.** You have stood by my side in ways only a daughter can. Your loyalty, love, and light inspire me every day, and I am deeply honored to call you mine.

With all my love and gratitude,
Dr. Michelle Stevens-Oldham

CONTENTS

INTERLUDE ONE

She Was My First Example"

In honor of Dr. Michelle Stevens-O
I never searched the world for a role model; I
was raised by one. Before the world introduced
me to women like Michelle Obama, I had
already seen grace in motion, integrity
embodied, and quiet strength wrapped in
wisdom and love.

She didn't wear a cape, but she rescued people.
She didn't build empires for fame, but she built
futures from broken places.

I watched her give beyond what was
comfortable, beyond what was easy. She opened
her doors to women with no shelter, fed children
who weren't her own, and taught the tired how
to stand again. And still, she never forgot who
she was becoming.

People call her many names: Doctor. Sister.
Auntie. Friend. But to me, she is Ma! The

woman who taught me that being soft is not weak, that working hard is an act of worship, and that lifting others is a sacred calling.

She poured into me, not with speeches, but with presence, not with perfection, but with power. The kind of power that mothers carry in their hands, the power to shape, nurture, and inspire.

If I stand tall today, it's because I saw her rise again and again, even when no one clapped. If I lead with courage, it's because I followed the example of her bold, prayerful steps.

She has done more good than can fit on any page, but the story lives on in me, in every strong decision I make, in every act of love I offer, in every dream I refuse to let die.

I am who I am, because she was who she is: My mother. My teacher. My first and forever role model.

I am Purposely
Ciara Stevens

About The Author

A Life of Purpose and Possibility

From humble beginnings to achieving dreams I once dared not imagine, my journey has been one of faith, resilience, and relentless pursuit of purpose. I am an author, a doctor of theology, a certified master life coach, an entrepreneur, a motivational speaker, an inventor, and a minister of the gospel. Each of these roles reflects a chapter in my life's story, one woven with challenges, triumphs, and unwavering commitment to helping others unlock their full potential.

The Power of the Written Word

Writing has always been a profound outlet for me, a way to express truths, inspire hearts, and leave a lasting impact. As the author of two books, "High Heels and Lip Stick" and "BootStraps and BowTies" I've had the privilege of sharing my experiences and insights with readers around the world. My words are born from lived realities, hard-won wisdom, and the desire to empower others to rise above life's difficulties. Each book is a testament to the strength of the human spirit and the transformative power of faith and perseverance.

A Scholar and Leader in Faith

Earning my doctorate in theology was not just an academic milestone but a spiritual awakening. It deepened my understanding of God's word and equipped me to minister effectively to others. My studies allowed me to explore complex theological concepts and apply them to real-world situations, providing guidance and hope to those seeking a deeper connection with their faith. As a minister of the gospel, I've had the honor of delivering messages that inspire transformation and healing, always grounded in the truth of scripture.

Coaching People to Greatness

As a certified master life coach, I have dedicated my life to helping individuals discover their purpose and navigate life's transitions. My coaching practice is rooted in the belief that everyone has untapped potential waiting to be unlocked. Whether it's guiding someone toward a career change, helping them overcome personal obstacles, or empowering them to dream bigger, my mission is to equip others with the tools they need to thrive.

Building Dreams as an Entrepreneur

Entrepreneurship has always been close to my heart. It's a space where creativity, strategy, and vision come together to create something meaningful. As a business owner, I've learned the importance of perseverance and adaptability. Building and leading my ventures has not only allowed me to provide for my family but has also been an avenue to create opportunities for others.

Inspiring Through Motivation

As a motivational speaker, I share my story and empower audiences to believe in themselves. My message is simple but profound: *Your past does not define you; your purpose does.* I've spoken to diverse groups, from aspiring entrepreneurs to those seeking spiritual renewal, always aiming to ignite the fire of possibility within them.

Innovating for a Better Future

As an inventor, I've embraced the challenge of turning ideas into tangible solutions. Innovation has taught me the value of thinking outside the box and finding creative ways to solve problems. It's a journey of trial and error, but one that mirrors the resilience required in life itself.

Ministering to the Soul

Above all, I am a minister of the gospel. This calling has been the foundation of everything I do. God's word is my greatest joy and responsibility. It reminds me daily that all my achievements are not just for my benefit but to serve others and glorify God.

Living a Life of Purpose

My life is a testament to the fact that no dream is too big, and no obstacle is insurmountable with faith, hard work, and perseverance. I hope my journey inspires others to chase their dreams relentlessly and to trust that their purpose is greater than their past. Every role I've embraced—author, scholar, coach, entrepreneur, speaker, inventor, and minister—is part of a larger mission: to uplift, inspire, and transform lives.

Loving You;

PSALMS 45:1

MY HEART IS OVERFLOWING WITH A
GOOD THEME'

I RECITE MY COMPOSITION
CONCERNING THE KING

MY TONGUE IS THE PEN OF A READY
WRITER

DEDICATION PAGE22

Job 40:10

"Adorn Yourself with Majesty and Dignity; Clothe Yourself with Glory and Splendor."

To all my beloved sisters and queens

This book is dedicated to you. You are resilient and radiant; you are the embodiment of strength, grace, and excellence. You are the dreamers, the builders, the nurturers, and the warriors who continue to rise despite every obstacle placed before you.

*You are not defined by the struggles you've faced but by the way you have **triumphed through them with dignity and grace.** We are unstoppable women, the living proof that beauty is not just seen, but felt, in the way we rise, evolve, and embrace our true selves. Like the black swan, you have defied expectations, stood in your power, and transformed every challenge into a masterpiece of triumph.*

May these pages serve as a reminder that your journey, your voice, and your presence are powerful beyond measure. Your beauty is not just in what the world sees, it is in your wisdom, your resilience, and your unbreakable spirit.

*This book is for you, the Black woman, for your unwavering courage, your boundless love, and the unshakable bond we share. **You are extraordinary, you are divine, and you are destined for greatness.** May you always walk boldly in your uniqueness, knowing that you are extraordinary, radiant, and deeply cherished.*

I write this from a place of love and admiration,
Dr. Michelle Stevens-O

FORWARD

In life's intricate tapestry, there are rare moments when paths cross at just the right time, creating space for deep transformation. My journey converged with **Dr. Michelle Stevens-O** during a season marked by time that, paradoxically, became rich soil for spiritual awakening and personal rediscovery.

Amid a circle of diverse women, we found unity through shared experiences, our stories weaving together beyond surface differences. In that sacred space, **Dr. Stevens-O**, a devoted minister and accomplished broadcast journalist, emerged as a guiding light. With grace and clarity, she nurtured our spirits while challenging us to grow. Her wisdom was not only spoken, it was lived. She didn't simply point to the path; she walked it with us, shining light ahead and holding us lovingly accountable as we pressed forward.

Throughout our time, we sojourned together, her steadfast commitment helped awaken in me the courage to stand on my own, to explore the depths of my identity, and to embrace my God-given gifts with purpose and boldness.

Now, with the release of her powerful work, *Beauty of the Black Swan*, Dr. Stevens-O once again calls women to healing and wholeness. This exquisite collection of poetry celebrates the complexity of womanhood, including the sacred, sensual spaces we often silence. It is both balm and mirror, a stirring testament to the resilience and beauty of Black women. Her words pour forth like a healing stream, refreshing the soul and reminding us of who we are.

As founder of **UBUNTU Publishing**, it is my profound honor to witness the birth of this work. I believe wholeheartedly that *Beauty of the Black Swan* will feed the spirits of women across generations, offering not just poetry but nourishment for the journey ahead.

With love, gratitude, and sisterhood,

Dr. Catinia Farrington

Founder and CEO, UBUNTU Publishing,

Clinical Psychologist and Holistic Life Coach,

Minister and Author

BEAUTY OF THE BLACK SWAN

Charm *is* deceitful and beauty *is* VAIN,
But a woman *who* fears the Lord, she
shall be praised **(Prov 31:30)**

MAJESTIC YOU CALL ME, YES, I AM AS
MAJESTIC AS CAN BE

I RISE AND SPREAD MY WINGS,

THE BEAUTY OF THE BLACK SWAN

LIKE A WOMAN MAJESTIC, FIERCE, HER
POWER GROWS.

A SOFTNESS IN THE WAY SHE FLOWS.

THE BEAUTY OF THE BLACK SWAN,

IT BENDS ITS ARCS IN FLUID GRACE,

IN EVERY BREATH SHE OWNS THE
SPACE.

THE BLACK SWAN GLIDES WHERE IN
ALL OF LIGHT'S CAPTIVITY,

A GRACE IN MOTION LIKE A DANCE
POISED IN THE FINEST SYMPHONY.

A MASTER'S PIECE,

OF NATURE'S ART,

HER BEAUTY OF WILD DECREE,

IN HER FLIGHT IT'S CAPTURED FOR THE
WORLD TO SEE.

SHE MOVES THROUGH LIFE, UNTAMED,
UNBOUND,

A QUEEN, A GODDESS DRAPED IN
TIMELESS LACE,

A QUIET STORM UPON HER FACE.

THE BEAUTY OF THE BLACK SWAN,

HER EYES LIKE STARS, REFLECT THE
NIGHT.

SHE HAS A SOUL SO STRONG

THAT CARRIES THE STRENGTH OF
HIDDEN MIGHT.

A SILHOUETTE OF PERFECT EASE,

WITH EACH STEP SHE TAKES WHISPERS
OF GRACE AND PEACE.

HER CURVES, A MYSTERY UNTOLD,

A VISION OF BEAUTY TO BEHOLD

A QUIET POWER, FIERCE AND STRONG,

YET SOFT LIKE A SILENT SONG.

IN EVERY BEAT IT OWNS THE SKIES,

WITH REGAL GRACE IT SOFTLY FLIES.

TO ANCIENT WINDS THAT GENTLY
SWEEP,

AS IF THE SKY ITSELF WANTS TO WEEP.

IN ALL IT'S BEAUTY, DYNAMIC YET
CALM,

IT STIRS THE SOUL LIKE A HEALING
BLAM.

THE BEAUTY OF THE BLACK SWAN

Psalm 96:6

SPLENDOR AND MAJESTY ARE
BEFORE HIM, STRENGTH AND
BEAUTY ARE IN HIS SANCTUARY

BEAUTY OF THE BLACK SWAN

Motivational Note

EACH OF US IS BORN A QUEEN! YOU ARE THE HIGHEST AUTHORITY UNDER GOD. ALL POWER RESTS WITHIN YOU.

IT'S UNDER THAT AUTHORITY IN WHICH YOU SPEAK. YOU CAN FORM YOUR LIFE HOWEVER YOU LIKE THE CHOICE IS YOURS.

SPEAK YOUR CIRCUMSTANCES

PROV 18:21- Death and life are in the power of the tongue: and they that love it shall eat the fruit thereof

WHERE YOU SIT, WHAT YOU STAND UP FOR! AND WHO YOU LAY WITH DETERMINES HOW YOU VIEW YOURSELF.

YOUR DECISIONS ALSO DICTATE THE THINGS YOU WILL EXPERIENCE.

BEAUTY OF THE BLACK SWAN

INTERLUDE 2

I put my pin to paper to describe this awesome woman,

Dr. Michelle Stevens-O, is a God-fearing woman whose faith is the cornerstone of her life. Her unwavering devotion to her beliefs shapes her every decision and inspires those around her. She possesses a nurturing spirit that manifests in her unwavering care for her family and anyone in need, yet she is a no-nonsense individual who values discipline and integrity. With a heart that balances compassion and firmness, she ensures those under her guidance are both loved and held accountable. Her transparency and honesty create a sense of trust, making her a beacon of truth in her community.

I have had the pleasure of knowing her for nearly twenty-one years, and she has always been transparent in any situation she may face.

Dr. Michelle exemplifies what it means to be a Proverbs 31 woman. Courage and intelligence define her character. She faces challenges head-on, guided by her faith and a sharp, analytical mind. Her wisdom and life experiences make her a source of inspiration for those seeking direction, and her words often carry the weight of transformative power. Whether standing firm in her convictions or extending a helping hand, she embodies the rare ability to lead with both strength and grace. Her life is a testament to the beauty of living boldly and authentically while remaining steadfastly rooted in love and faith.

Linda Nichols

THE FABRIC OF A BLACK WOMAN

I WAS CREATED BY THE SPIRIT OF GOD. WONDERFULLY AND MARVELOUSLY MADE. WITH A HEART BEAT LIKE THE SOUND OF A DRUM, BOOM, BOOM, BOOM BOOM, BOOM. **THE FABRIC OF A BLACK WOMAN**

BLACK, MULATTO, NEGRO, COLORED, BLACK AMERICAN, AFRICAN AMERICAN. SOME HATE ME, SOME RAPE ME, SOME DATE ME, SOME LOVE ME. THEY WANT TO TASTE ME, FEEL ME, BUT! THEY REALLY WANT TO BEHOLD ME. **THE FABRIC OF A BLACK WOMAN**

MY SKIN IS AS BLACK AS COLE, ONYX, BROWN AS MILK CHOCOLATE, WHITE ALBANO LIKE SATIN. SOME TAN FOR IT, SOME LAY IN THE SUN AND BURN FOR IT. BUT JUST WAIT IT WILL FADE. ONLY MY MELANIN SKIN TONE WILL LAST. **THE FABRIC OF A BLACK WOMAN**

THEY SAY YOUR EYES ARE THE WINDOW TO YOUR SOUL. MINE ARE BLACK, BROWN, BLUE, HAZEL, GRAY, AND GREEN. WHAT I SEE IS THE DIVINE

PROVIDENCE BEYOND CREATION. **THE FABRIC OF A BLACK WOMAN**

MY VOICE IS STRONG LIKE THUNDER, IT'S SOFT WITH THE MIXTURE OF SOUND AND TONES THAT MAKE SENTENCES FLOW, THAT CREATE BEAUTIFUL PHRASES, PARAGRAPHS, MELODIES, AND IS DYNAMIC, THAT WILL MAKE YOU STAND AND TAKE NOTICE. **THE FABRIC OF A BLACK WOMAN**

MY BACK IS STRONG, I CARRY THE HISTORY OF MY ANCESTORS AND THE WEIGHT OF MY CHILD AS HE RIDE, BECAUSE HE DOESN'T WANT TO WALK. MY SOUL IS THE EMOTIONAL, INTELLECTUAL ENERGY AND INTENSITY OF A PIECE OF ARTISTIC PERFORMANCE. **THE FABRIC OF A BLACK WOMAN**

MY HAIR IS SOFT, LONG, SHORT, CURLY, AND WOOLY TOO. IT'S A BEAUTY NO ONE CAN OUTDO. I AM CAPTIVATING AND THE ESSENCE OF BEAUTY, I AM AMBITIOUS, I AM CONFIDENT, I AM THE VALUE THAT'S IMMEASURABLE, I SET THE STANDARDS FOR CLASSY. **THE FABRIC OF A BLACK WOMAN**

MY ARMS ARE STRONG AS I PUSH THROUGH THE PRESSURE OF THE WORLD, THE FORCE OF NATURE, AND EVERY CHALLENGE I MEET, AS I JOURNEY THROUGH THIS LIFE. **THE FABRIC OF A BLACK WOMAN**

MY LOVE IS PRECIOUS, MY LOVE IS STRONG, MY LOVE IS PASSIONATE. I EMBODY RELIANT LOVE, I'M THERE WHEN YOU NEED ME AND I'M THERE WHEN YOU DON'T. MY LOVE IS RESILIENT; MY LOVE IS INVITING AND ALL EMCOMPASSING. **THE FABRIC OF A BLACK WOMAN**

MY LEGS AND FEET HOLD ME UP AS I LEAVE MY FOOTPRINTS OF FAILURES AND ACHIEVEMENTS, AS I MAKE MY MARK IN TIME THAT NEVER STAND STILL. I AM THE EXISTENCE AND CREATION OF **THE FABRIC OF A BLACK WOMAN**

CALL ME DESIRE

I AM THE POWER THAT NO MAN CAN
SEE,
I CAN CONTROL THE UNIVERSE AND ALL
HUMANITY.

I AM DESIRE

I AM A VESSEL SOFT, YET STRONG,
A FORCE OF PASSION WRAPPED WITHIN,
IT MOVES LIKE FIRE BENEATH YOUR
SKIN

I SATISFY YOUR DEEPEST CRAVINGS
AND GIVE PLEASURE TO YOUR
GREATEST URGE;
I MAKE MEN SHAKE AND RATTLE THEIR
EVERY NERVE

THE SPACE THAT HOUSE ME,
IS TO SOME STILL A MYSTERY

I HAVE BROUGHT MEN TO TEARS
AND BECAUSE OF ME,
WOMEN HAVE LEARNED OF THEIR
GREATEST FEARS.

I AM DESIRE

MEN HAVE A NEED TO TOUCH ME,
FEEL ME
AND SOME SET THEIR TONGUE UPON
MY LIPS TO TASTE ME

IT'S STRONG ENOUGH TO BREAK ANY
BOND
AND BEND ANY WILL,
IT MAKES YOU HAVE A DEEP HUNGER
AND A QUIET THRILL.

THEY CALL ME DESIRE

IN ITS HEAT WE FIND A PLACE,
WHERE BODY, SOUL, AND HEART
EMBRACE

I HOLD LIFE IN MY HAND,
IN ME BIRTH IS PRESENT IN ALL THE
LAND

I LAY IN THE MIDDLE OF THE GARDEN,
I AM THE TREE OF LIFE,
DESIRE THEY CALL ME

I CAN BLOW YOUR MIND
AND CONTROL YOU TOO,

I CAN MAKE YOU DO WHATEVER I
COMMAND OF YOU

I AM THE CHERRY THAT POP,
I AM THE CREAM OF THE CROP

IN MY PULSE A RHYTHM WILD,
I'M POWERFUL ENOUGH TO MAKE THE
STRONGEST MAN MILD

I CAUSE WARS LIKE A SAVAGE FLAME,
A FORCE OF NATURE,
I CONTROL KINGDOMS AND MAKE
THEM TAMED

THEY CALL ME DESIRE

A POWERFUL TOUCH,
YET SOFT AND FREE,
MY CURVES,
MY PATHS A DEEP, DEEP MYSTERY

I AM LUSCIOUS,
I AM HOT,
ONLY THE KING OF GLORY MAY ENTER
THIS SPOT

THEY CALL ME DESIRE

EXCEPTIONAL LOVE

IT'S EXOTIC, EXCEPTIONAL

A LOVE SO DEEP IT MAKES YOU
EMOTIONAL

I LOVE YOU WITH AN EVERLASTING
LOVE,

A LOVE SO DEEP IT CONSUMES YOUR
SOUL,

RIGHT BEFORE YOUR EYES,

THIS STORY UNFOLDS

THIS LOVE WILL MAKE YOU CLIMB THE
HIGHEST MOUNTAIN,

AND SWIM THE DEEPEST SEA,

IT WILL MAKE YOU RUN TO THE END OF
THE EARTH SEARCHING FOR ME

EXCEPTIONAL LOVE CAPTIVATES YOU,

THIS LOVE MOST SEEK,

OTHERS DESIRE TO REACH SUCH A PEAK

THIS LOVE MOVES LIKE THE SILENT
WIND,

YET STRONG, UNTAMED,

IT ENGULFS YOUR ENTIRE FRAME

YOU ARE MY ONE AND ONLY,

MY LOVE IS SO EXCEPTIONAL

YOU WILL NEVER BE LONELY

THIS LOVE IS SO STRONG

WHEN YOU CAN'T THINK STRAIGHT,

I JAY WALK ACROSS YOUR MIND,

IT MAKES YOU SHAKE,

QUIVER AND EVERYTHING BECOMES
UNWIND

I GIVE MY LOVE EXCEPTIONALLY,

FROM THE START, TO PART FROM ME,

COULD CAUSE GREAT PAIN AND DEEP
DEEP HURT IN YOUR HEART

EXCEPTIONAL LOVE,

GIVES YOU A WORLD WIND OF
EMOTIONS,

IT SETS YOU AT SEA LIKE A BOAT ON AN
UNSTEADY OCEAN

THIS LOVE IS NOT ORDINARY, IT MAKES
YOU SING OOH LA LA, IN THE MORNING
AND IN THE NIGHT, OOH LA LA, IT'S
EXTRAORDINARY

IT WILL MAKE YOU CROSS THE
DESSERT;

IT WILL MAKE YOU CHASE THE SUN,

IT WILL MAKE YOU BELIEVE THE
IMPOSSIBLE CAN BE DONE

IT'S EXCEPTIONAL YOU SEE,

IT WILL MAKE YOU LOSE YOUR MIND
OVER ME

IT'S THE SPARK THAT LIGHTS YOUR
NIGHT,

IT MAKES YOUR HEART SKIP A BEAT,

IT WILL MAKE YOU RUN AND TAKE A
FLIGHT,

EVEN IF YOU HAVE TO TAKE THE LAST
SEAT

IT'S A UNIVERSE MADE JUST FOR TWO,

YOU WILL SCALE EVERY BRIDGE,

YOU WILL LET NOTHING BLOCK YOUR
VIEW.

BECAUSE YOU KNOW THIS LOVE IS
PURE AND TRUE

EXCEPTIONAL LOVE

1PETER 2:9

BUT YOU ARE A CHOSEN GENERATION, A
ROYAL PRIESTHOOD,

A HOLY NATION, HIS SPECIAL PEOPLE,

THAT YOU MAY PROCLAIM THE PRAISES
OF HIM

WHO CALLED YOU OUT OF DARKNESS

INTO HIS MARVELOUS LIGHT

INTERLUDE 3

Dr. Michelle Stevens-O

Over the years, I have watched in awe as you have faced life's challenges with unwavering bravery, rising time and time again with grace and determination. Your ability to dream, even in the face of uncertainty, and to create beauty from the fragments of the past is nothing short of inspiring.

You have a remarkable gift for turning hope into reality, seeing possibilities where others see limits, and building a future that reflects your passion, vision, and courage.

Truthfully, my love and admiration go deeper than words could ever express, so I will honor you with my sincerest friendship and always see the purpose and divinity in you.

TaJuana Adeshina Burley

ME, MYSELF AND I

ME,
I AM THE CREATION OF MARVELOUS
EXPRESSION. CAUSING GREAT WONDER,

ME, MYSELF, AND I.

WITH EVERY PAIN AND EVERY PUSH,
YOU HEAR THE SOUND OF THUNDER.

I CAME FORTH LIKE LIGHTNING,
LIGHTING UP THE SKY CAUSING A
COSMIC EFFECT,
A SIGHT OF BEAUTY TO BEHOLD.
WITH ENOUGH POWER TO CAUSE GREAT
DESTRUCTION.

I AM POETIC,

A PIECE OF MELODY,
LIKE A SONG THAT YOU HUM WHEN
LOVE FILLS YOUR SOUL
YOU CAN FEEL IT, YOU CAN HEAR IT.
I AM THE URGE YOU NEED TO PUT THE
FIRE OUT THAT BURNS DEEP INSIDE.

I WALK BY FAITH,
I TOLD MYSELF, YOU, MUST LOVE, YOU!

I AM MIND-BLOWING,
I CAN ACHIEVE THE IMPOSSIBLE,
ALWAYS WEARING A SMILE,
RUNNING FREE, RUNNING WILD.
LIKE STANDING ON A CLIFF,
I FEEL THE WIND BENEATH MY FEET.

SOME ARE DRAWN TO WHAT I KNOW
AND SOME ARE DRAWN TO WHAT I DO,
BUT THEY ARE OBLIVIOUS TO WHO I AM,

ME, MYSELF, AND I.
I AM PRICELESS.

IT'S THE ME INSIDE THAT CHALLENGES
THE WORLD.
I HAVE BEEN THROUGH MANY
CHALLENGES AND SOME HAVE FELT
LIKE BATTLES,
BUT I COULD NOT QUIT.

I REALIZE MY DESTINY IS WORTH
FIGHTING FOR.
I'M NOT FIGHTING FOR SOMETHING
INCONSEQUENTIAL, OR IRRELEVANT,
BUT FOR MY OWN MEANINGFUL AND
WORTHWHILE PURPOSE.

I AM EPIC EXPRESSION,
THE COLOR OF LOVE AND BREATH
TAKEN.
I HAVE A PREDESTINED PURPOSE,
I AM A CHAMPION,
AND I OVERCOME EVERY ADVERSITY.

ME, MYSELF, AND I,
I AM ENOUGH!

I DON'T LET OTHERS DEFINE ME, OR
HOW I SEE MYSELF,
THEY LOOK THROUGH STAINED
COLORED LENSES.
I AM MANY FACETS,
AN UNDEFINABLE ASPECT OF ME,
MYSELF, AND I

I AM!

I AM BOUNDLESS ABUNDANCE AND
RADIANT EXPRESSION.
I AM LIKE THE MOON THAT GLOWS AT
NIGHT AND THE SUN THAT LIGHTS THE
WORLD,

I AM FEARLESS.

WHEN I LOOK IN THE MIRROR, THE
REFLECTION I SEE IS THE IMAGE OF
GOD.
ME, MYSELF AND I.

THE ESSENCE OF A WOMAN

I AM THAT I AM,

THE ESSENCE OF BEAUTY,

CREATED BY AN INTRINSIC NATURE OF
INDISPENSABLE QUALITY

WITH AN ORA THAT FILLS THE AIR WITH
AN AROMA OF LUXURY

HER SKIN HAS THE TOUCH OF SATIN
THAT LAYS LIKE ROLLING WAVES

HER SOUL IS BOUNDLESS, TIMELESS,
BRAVE AND WHOLE.

IT'S DEFINED AND CREATED BY GOD,

DRAFTED BY HIS DIVINE LOVE IN A
MOMENT NO MAN WILL EVER
UNDERSTAND

THE BLOOD IN HER VEINS IS SCARLET
RED,

HER BEAUTY, HER ESSENCE COMMAND
ATTENTION LIKE THE TURNING OF
HEADS

THE CURVE OF HER NECK, DELICATE
AND TENDER,

A GRACEFUL LINE ON GENTLE HANDS.

IT COMMANDS NOTICE,

ALL HEADS TURN IN ADMIRATION AND
ADULATION

THE SOFTNESS OF HER BREAST WHERE
BABIES REST

DRIPS THE OIL OF LIFE AND EVEN GIVES
MEN DELIGHT

HER ARMS ARE STRONG MADE TO HOLD
YOU AND EMBRACE YOU

DESIGNED TO HELP AND CARRY YOU
THROUGH

THE ESSENCE OF A WOMAN

THE STRENGTH OF HER SPINE
IS UNYIELDING

WITH EVERY TRIAL SHE'S REBORN

A FORCE OF MIGHT, A QUIET STORM

THE ESSENCE OF A WOMAN

HER GRACE IS LIKE A PUFF OF PERFUME
THAT FLOWS LIKE A RIVER WIDE

AS SHE MOVES, SHE CARRIES THE
WAVES OF THE OCEAN IN HER STRIDE

SHE IS THE EARTH, SKY, AND SEA

HER ESSENCE IS THE BEAUTY OF ALL
ETERNITY

THE ESSENCE OF A WOMAN

FORBIDDEN

I LONG FOR YOU,

AND I DON'T DESIRE ANOTHER,

YOUR LOVE IS SEDUCTIVE,

I CRAVE FOR IT,

YOU HAVE FULL CONTROL OF ME,

AND I AM A SLAVE FOR IT

HIS HANDS THEY ROAM,

THEY CLAIM MY SOUL,

HE'S A HUSBAND,

I STEAL AND BE STOLE

HE WEARS A RING,

A GOLDEN TIE,

WHEN WE'RE TOGETHER IT HAS NO
MEANING,

I TURN A BLIND EYE

I'M THE SECRET HE CAN'T CONFESS,
HE'S MY ESCAPE, HIS LOVE IS THE BEST

IN HIS EMBRACE,

I'M FREE YET CHAINED,

CAPTIVE TO LOVE THAT'S JOY AND PAIN

FORBIDDEN

YES

HIS TOUCH IGNITES MY FLAME,

HE'S FORBIDDEN

AND I'M JUST A SHADOW IN HIS NAME

ACROSS THE ROOM HE CAPTURES MY
GAZE,

THE STRENGTH OF MY DESIRE SETS ME
ABLAZE,

EACH RENDEZVOUS A BORROWED
BLISS,

EACH STOLEN HOUR A MUCH-NEEDED
KISS

SHADOWS STRETCH AND TRUTH
EMERGE,

MY GUILT AND MY HUNGER FIERCELY
SURGE

YOU BELONG TO HER,

SHE WAITS FOR YOU,

UNSEEN, UNHEARD, UNTOUCHED BY
YOU,

A LOVE LIKE THIS THOUGH SWEET,

IS CRUEL,

A WICKED GAME OF TWO FOOLS

FORBIDDEN

HIS WORDS, A CASCADE OF LIES HE
TELLS,

LIKE THOSE WHISPERED VOWS,

DECEPTION BLOOMS,

HELPLESS TO THIS MOMENT, I ALLOW

A PASSION THAT DEEPLY CALLS,

THE STING OF HIS SWEET LUST,

EACH STOLEN MOMENT A GOLDEN
PRIZE,

THE BURNING TRUTH WE CANNOT
DISGUISE

BOUND TO ANOTHER WHO CARRIES
YOUR NAME,
I'M THE DISTANT TROPHY IN THIS
CRUEL LOVE GAME
FORBIDDEN

IF SHE KNEW WHAT YOU DO TO ME,
AND WHAT I DO TO YOU,
IN YOUR ARMS THE WORLD DISSOLVES,
I AM LOST, MY SINS ABSOLVE

I'M THE BEAUTY OF A SHADOW,
IN YOUR BRIGHT LIT DAY,
THE SEXUAL DESIRE IN YOUR DREAMS
THAT'S FLEETING,
I CANNOT STAY

ALTHOUGH YOU ARE MY HEARTBEAT
WILD AND TRUE,

YOU BELONG TO ANOTHER AND SHE
BELONGS TO YOU

YOUR TOUCH IS FIRE,

DESIRE IT BURNS,

IT BRANDS,

A FORBIDDEN HEAT,

I CAN'T WITHSTAND,

NO GUILT, A SPECTER, HAUNTS THE AIR,

A SILENT WITNESS TO OUR LOVE AFFAIR

FORBIDDEN

PSALM 145:1-3

I WILL EXTOL YOU, MY GOD, O'KING

AND I WILL BLESS YOUR NAME
FOREVER AND EVER.

EVERYDAY I WILL BLESS YOU,

AND I WILL PRAISE YOUR NAME
FOREVER AND EVER

GREAT IS THE LORD, AND GREATLY TO
BE PRAISED;

AND HIS GREATNESS IS UNSEARCHABLE

INTERLUDE 4

Dr. Michelle Stevens O.

Is truly a remarkable individual, embodying strength, beauty, and intentionality in all aspects of her life. Her dedication to her professional pursuits is matched only by her passion for empowering other women. Through various initiatives and projects, she has demonstrated an unwavering commitment to helping others unlock their potential and pursue their passions.

Her resourceful mindset allows her to approach challenges with creativity and determination, finding innovative solutions and inspiring those around her. Her ability to think quickly on her feet not only showcases her adaptability but also highlights her leadership qualities.

She serves as a role model for many, proving that success is about personal achievement and lifting others as you rise.

Dr. Michelle's influence extends beyond her professional accomplishments, as she continues to motivate and inspire countless individuals on their journey toward empowerment and self-discovery.

Undeniably A Queen!

Coach Yava "LaTrice" Harris-Swearington-

B.A Psychology

PRETTY IS AS PRETTY DOES

CHARM IS DECEITFUL, AND BEAUTY IS
VAIN, THIS WOMAN IS TO BE ADMIRED
AND PRAISED

SHE IS INTELLECTUAL, SEXUAL,
SENSITIVE, AND GENTLE TOO

SHE WALKS WITH GRACE
HER HEAD HELD HIGH,
A SPARK OF FIRE IN HER EYE

HER GENTLE VOICE CAN SOOTHE THE
ROARING LION AND CALM THE BEAST
INSIDE,
SHE'S ALWAYS ON READY,
WHEN THE FIGHT BREAKS OUT, SHE'LL
BE BY YOUR SIDE

HER SASS IS SHARP
A PLAYFUL TEASE,
QUICK WITH HER WIT,
FIERCE WITH AN ARTFUL EASE,

PRETTY IS AS PRETTY DOES

HER STRENGTH IS UNYIELDING,
FORGED IN FIRE,

THE WARRIOR INSIDE,
SHE'S CAPABLE,
A FORCE UNSEEN,
SMALL IN STATURE, MIGHTY IN POWER,
SHE FIGHTS WITH HER LEFT HAND AND
BUILDS THE WALL OF PROTECTION
WITH HER RIGHT

DON'T BE FOOLED BY THE HEAT SHE
BRINGS
FOR PRETTY ISN'T JUST A FACE,
IT'S HOW SHE MOVES, WITH
BOUNDLESS GRACE

HER WORDS ARE STEEL THAT CUT LIKE
A SHARP BLADE,
SHE IS SASSY, SHE IS STRONG, SHE
WALKS IN A CLASS ALL HER OWN

SHE IS DOWN FOR THE FIGHT AND UP
FOR THE WIN,
WHEN THE GOING GETS TOUGH, WITH
SHEAR DETERMINATION THIS LADY
JUMPS IN

PRETTY IS AS PRETTY DOES!

WITH SWAY IN HER HIPS,
AN AIR OF CONFIDENCE IN HER STRIDE,

SHE IS FABULOUS, MARVELOUS, AND
INDESCRIBABLE TOO,
SHE'S COURAGEOUS, CLAD IN SILKEN
HUE

HER HEART, LIFE TRIALS HAVE
SCORCHED,
STILL DARES TO BEAT,
IT HAS RHYTHM BOTH CRUEL AND
SWEET,
STAND IN AWE, FOR SHE'S DIVINE,
A SOUL WHERE BEAUTY AND STRENGTH
COMBINE

PRETTY IS AS PRETTY DOES

SHE LOVES WITH FORCE AS STRONG
HAS HATE,
SHE HAS A PASSION YOU CAN NOT
ESCAPE,

HER RAGE IS DEEP
HER WORDS ARE SHARP,
HER TOUCH CAN HEAL,
HER TOUCH CAN STING,
THERE'S A PARADOX IN EVERYTHING

PRETTY IS AS PRETTY DOES

SHE'S POWERED BY HER HOPES AND
HER DREAMS,
SHE HAS A WINNERS QUALITY,
THE POWER TO HOLD ON,
THE POWER TO ENDURE
THE HUNGER TO FACE DEFEAT,
IN THAT SHE'S SURE

PRETTY IS AS PRETTY DOES

SHE'S IN CONTROL, OF EVERYTHING
SHE DOES,
IT IS MASSIVE, ENORMOUS, COLOSSAL
TOO,
HER MAKEUP FLAWLESS,
HER CURLS FLOWING,
HER LOUIS VUITTONS WILL NOT DUE

HER POWER TO SUCCEED,
AND HER ACHE TO ACHIEVE,
PUSHES THIS LADY UP THE LADDER TO
IT'S HIGHEST PEAK

SHE WALKS IN BEAUTY, BOLD AND
RARE,
WATCHING EACH STEP CAREFUL NOT TO
FALL,
CROWNED WITH GLORY

SHE DOESN'T JUST SURVIVE, SHE
THRIVES,
MANY WOMEN HAVE DONE WELL, BUT
YOU EXCEL THEM ALL
PRETTY IS AS PRETTY DOES

SECRETS

A REBEL SHOUTS IN ANGER,
A WISE MAN HOLDS HIS TONGUE
AND CALM TAKES CONTROL

THERE ARE TRUTHS THAT BLOOM,
YET NEVER TAKE FLIGHT,
BOUND TO MY MIND,
HIDDEN OUT OF SIGHT

SECRETS

I HAVE STORIES THAT'S NEVER BEEN
TOLD,
IF REVEALED WILL BE LIKE A SCOLDING
THAT UNFOLDS

THESE TRUTHS ARE MINE,
NO EARS MAY HEAR, NO LIPS MAY
SPEAK
FOR THE COST OF TELLING, FEELS FAR
TOO STEEP

THEY PULSE FOR LIFE,
THEY ACHE, THEY BURN,
YEARNING FOR FREEDOM
BUT WITH REASON I DISCERN

FOR FEAR THEY LINGER
A GHOSTLY CHAIN,
BINDING MY THOUGHTS IN SILENCE
AND IN PAIN

BENEATH THE SURFACE,
LIES A WORLD OF SECRETS I DARE NOT
SAY,
WITH A SMILE ON MY FACE,
UNDER THE MASK I WEAR DAY BY DAY

I WEAR MY CHARM LIKE MORTAL
DISPLAY,
WRAPPED UP IN THIS BALL OF HUMAN
CLAY

I LONG TO SPEAK,
TO SET THEM FREE,
TO LET THE WORLD KNOW ALL OF ME

BUT I GUARD MY HEART,
I SEAL MY LIPS,
I WALK IN SILENCE LIKE A SAILING SHIP

I HOLD MY HEAD,
SCREAMING INSIDE,
I TELL MYSELF, EVERY SECRET YEARNS
TO FLY,
EVERY FEAR MUST SAY GOODBYE

WILL COURAGE RISE,
WILL I FIND STRENGTH IN MY HEART,
WILL I BE BOLD ENOUGH TO TELL
EVERY PART

EACH WORD UNSAID,
EACH LINE A TETHERED THREAD,
EACH TRUTH SUPPRESSED
FEELS LIKE A GUN HELD TO MY HEAD
A STORY WHISPERED,
NEVER FULLY TOLD,
THERE'S A WEIGHT I CARRY TO HEAVY
TO HOLD

THESE SECRETS OF MINE,
THEY CLING THEY BIND
EACH COMPLICATED THOUGHT LOCKED
WITHIN MY MIND

THE FEAR THAT LOOMS,
LIKE A TOWERING WALL
WHAT IF I'M JUDGED,
WHAT WOULD THEY SAY IF I FALL

WHAT IF MY TRUTHS UNRAVEL ME,
WHAT IF THEY LEAVE ME BARE FOR THE
WORLD TO SEE

FEAR HOLD ME WITH COLD HANDS
GRIPPED SO TIGHT,
SO UNKIND,
I HAVE A QUIET WAR RAGING IN MY
MIND

SOMETIMES MERE WORDS ARE NOT
ENOUGH
THERE'S A NEED INSIDE TO STAND AND
BE TOUGH

SO I KEEP MY SECRETS BURIED DEEP
WITHIN,
HOLDING THEM SO TIGHT,
NOT EVEN THE DARK OF NIGHT HAS A
CHANCE TO CREEP IN
SECRETS

STORM

I AM LIKE A VIOLENT RUCKUS,
CREATING A BEAUTIFUL DISTURBANCE
IN THE ATMOSPHERE

WITH BOOMING RAYS AND
THUNDEROUS SOUND,
IT STIRS THE SKIES AND SHAKES THE
GROUND

MY STRONG WINDS ARE BOLD ENOUGH
TO MOVE MOUNTAINS AND DIVIDE THE
LAND,
IT'S LIKE HANDLING THE DELICATE
HEART WITH AN UNSETTLED HAND

A NOISY FIGHT, A COMMOTION THAT
ROARS IN THE MIND,
THE WINDS OF DOUBT THAT WHISPER
LOUD,
AN UNSETTLED CHAOS I LEAVE BEHIND

AS I SWEEP THE LAND AND TEAR
THROUGH TREES,
I'M LIKE A CHAOTIC BAND WILD AND
FREE

I BRING FORTH WINDS,

THEY HOWL, TWIST, AND BEND,
I CAN MAKE YOU DANCE TO ANY SONG
WITHOUT AN END

I SEND THUNDEROUS ROARS IN YOUR
MIND,
CLEARING THE CHAOS THE WORLD
LEFT BEHIND,
THE LIGHTNING STRIKE,
A BLINDING FLARE,
A JAGGED LINE THAT SCORCHES THE
AIR
A WHISPER YOU CAN HEAR,
A SHOUT, A TEAR
I MAKE THINGS TWIST, AND SHIFT,
AS FAST AS I COME, I DISAPPEAR

I SCATTER PIECES ONE BY ONE,
IT'S LIKE A PUZZLE,
YOUR MIND, I LEAVE UNDONE

WHILE IN THE EYE FEELINGS ARE
PULLED,
WINDS OF WORRY TWIST AND SCREAM,
I CAN SHAKE THE FOUNDATION OF THE
HAPPIEST DREAM

THERE'S BEAUTY IN THIS UNCERTAINTY,
STORM,

CHANGING THE COURSE OF YOUR
DESTINY

HOLD TO YOUR SEAT, GRAB THE BAR,
I'M STORM,
EMOTIONS RISE THEN FALL AWAY,
UNSETTLED AND LOST WITHOUT MUCH
TO SAY

THE SKIES WILL CLEAR,
THE CALM WILL COME,
THE EMOTIONAL STORM WILL SOON BE
DONE
ALTHOUGH IT LEFT THE LAND
UNSETTLED AND TORN,
THERE'S A BEAUTY THAT COMES AFTER
THE STORM

STORM

PSALM 139:14

I WILL PRAISE YOU

FOR I AM FEARFULLY AND
WONDERFULLY MADE

MARVELOUS ARE YOUR WORKS

AND THAT MY SOUL KNOWS VERY
WELL

INTERLUDE 5

It is with great joy and deep honor that I share these words.

Dr. Michelle Stevens-O has been a cherished part of my life for over twenty-five years. I still remember the first time we met; she greeted me with warmth, joy, and open arms, her spirit radiating love. She was singing a gospel song and quoting scripture, referencing the blessing of a man finding a good wife. That moment captured her essence: vibrant, faith-filled, and full of purpose.

As the years unfolded, I came to know the depth of her character and the breadth of her gifts. Dr. Stevens-O is a true visionary, **a serial entrepreneur** whose mind is always in motion, constantly creating, building, and pursuing new opportunities. Her passion for **uplifting women of all backgrounds** is evident in everything she does. Whether through her words, her work, or her presence, she has encouraged me many times and offered wisdom that I still carry with me today.

I have watched her rise through life's challenges with grace and unshakable faith. Time and again, she has faced adversity head-on, never allowing trials to break her spirit. Instead, she climbs each mountain with strength and determination, **a living testament to what it means to be unstoppable**.

Dr. Michelle wears many hats, each one worn with excellence. She is a **God-fearing woman**, strong-minded and committed to seeing things through. She is a gifted counselor, a loyal friend, a powerful writer, a poetic soul, and a source of unwavering support. As a **sister, sister-in-law, and sister-in-love**, she brings love, light, and wisdom into every relationship she nurtures.

I am truly **blessed** beyond words to call her my sister-in-love. Her life inspires, her presence uplifts, and her faith leads the way.

Mrs. Marcia May

I'M BLACK, I'M A WOMAN

I'M BLACK AND I'M PROUD AND I SAY IT
VERY LOUD
MY SKIN A CANVAS RICH AND BOLD,
I'M A TRUE STORY NOW TO BE UNFOLD.

I RISE LIKE THE MORNING SUN,
A FORCE OF NATURE,
SECOND TO NONE.

WITH EVERY STEP AND EVERY STRIDE,
THE EARTH RUMBLES AND IT SHAKES,
I CAUSE THE DIRT UNDER THE WATERS
TO BREAK.

I DANCE THROUGH THE STRUGGLES,
I GAIN STRENGTH WITH EVERY PAIN,
WITH EVERY SETBACK I RISE AGAIN
AND AGAIN

I AM BLACK, I'M A WOMAN

WITH ROOTS SO DEEP RUNNING
THROUGH HISTORY'S PAGES,
MY SPIRITS STRONG AND FREE,
I'M LIKE THE FINEST WINE,
I NEVER AGE,
I GET BETTER WITH TIME.

I'M LIKE A TORNADO, FIERCE AND FREE,
MY STRENGTH AND COURAGE
IS LIKE AN ORCHESTRA PLAYING THE
FINEST SYMPHONY

I'M BLACK AND I'M PROUD AND I SAY IT
VERY LOUD

I BIRTH A NATION,
I BUILD FROM ASHES,
AND I CARVE FROM STONE,
A KINGDOM, A WORLD NO ONE DARES
TO OWN

I AM THE ESSENCE OF STRENGTH

I'M THE REFLECTION OF MY WARRIOR
SISTERS
AND MANY MOTHER QUEENS,
EVERY MAN I BIRTH WAS BORN A KING

I'M BLACK I'M A WOMAN

I SAY IT LOUD, I'M BLACK AND I'M
PROUD

MY VOICE IS LIKE A DRUMBEAT,
CLEAR AND STRONG,

WITH EVERY WORD OF INSTRUCTIONS
YOU WILL NEVER GO WRONG

I LIVE IN AN ANTHEM OF SILENCE,
I HAVE A LOVE SO PURE,
I HAVE A STRENGTH WITHIN THAT
HELPS YOU TO ENDURE

MY LOVE HEALS ALL,
MY TEARS BRING RAIN,
MY NAME IS WRITTEN IN THE BOOK OF
LIFE,
IN THE HALL OF FAME

MY SKIN SO DARK YOU CALL ME
BLACKY,
MY SKIN SO LIGHT BRIGHT,
YOU TRY TO SEPARATE ME,
OTHERS TRY TO BE LIKE ME,
I AM THE TRUTH.
I AM THE STANDARD,
I'M THE CREAM OF CROP,
I AM A MIC DROP

THE POWER THAT HOLD ME UP,
IT'S CALLED A SPINE,
I HAVE A FORCE OF NATURE NO WORDS
CAN DEFINE

I'M A MOTHER,
A LEADER,
A QUEEN, AND A FRIEND,
I HAVE A STRENGTH, I DON'T BREAK,
I JUST BEND

MY EYES,
THE TWO PEARLS THAT SEE,
HAVE WITNESSED DREAMS PASS AND
ALL OF LIFE'S MYSTERY

I WALK WITH A RHYTHM THAT MOVES
THE GROUND,
A MELODY OF STRENGTH, WHERE
GRACE IS FOUND

I SAY IT OUT LOUD, I'M BLACK AND I'M
PROUD
MY SPIRIT IS FIRE,
MY SOUL A FLAME,
I SET THE COURSE OF NATURE THAT
BUILDS TO FRAME

ON EVERY CORNER MY NAME IS
CALLED,
MY NAME ON LIPS LIKE A SONG THAT
ECHOS AND FALL

I MOVE WITH SUCH ELEGANCE AND I
MOVE WITH GRACE,
I BREAK THROUGH CEILINGS, AND I
BEND THE BARS OF CHALLENGES I FACE

I HAVE FAME,
I HAVE POWER,
I HAVE BEAUTY,
SO SPEAK OF THIS BLACK WOMAN WITH
CARE,
I JUST MAY BE THE ANSWER TO YOUR
PRAYER

I'M BLACK, I'M A WOMAN
I'M BLACK AND I'M PROUD AND I SAY IT
VERY LOUD

THE UNTOUCHABLE LOVE

I LONG FOR YOU,
MY LOVE IS A VIOLIN
THAT YOU STRUM,
IT'S BREATH-TAKING.

I AM LIKE A BLAZE,
A GOLDEN AMBER,
WARM AND GENTLE,
YET POWERFUL ENOUGH TO ENGULF
YOU.

UNTOUCHABLE LOVE

MY LOVE IS LIKE THE SUNRISE AND
KISSES THE DAY,
IT'S LIKE THE FALL OF DEW AS IT KISSES
THE EARTH
MY LOVE IS SO INTENSE, IT'S
IRRESISTIBLE.

MY LOVE IS SO STRONG
THAT MY SOUL SEEKS TO TOUCH YOU IN
THE DEEPEST PARTS.
I LOVE YOU WITH AN EVERLASTING
LOVE.
WHO DOES NOT KNOW LOVE,
FOR GOD IS LOVE.

I AM UNTOUCHABLE LOVE.
MY LOVE ABIDES IN THE OCEAN
CURRENT,
THAT CREATES THE GREATEST WAVES,
NO HANDS CAN GRASP,
NO EYE CAN SEE
THE BOUNDLESS DEPTHS OF THIS
MYSTERY.

UNTOUCHABLE LOVE.

IN MIDNIGHT,
WHERE SHADOWS PLAY,
MY LOVE IS LIKE A FORCE UNSEEN,
YET FELT SO DEEP,
PULLING ME THROUGH THE REALMS
UNKNOWN,
WHERE TIME AND DREAMS RUN FREE.

I LOSE MYSELF IN UNTOUCHABLE LOVE,
WHERE THE WORLD DISSOLVES IN
SILENCE,
AS YOU BECOME MY ALL,
A UNIVERSE WHERE LOVE RISES AND
FALLS

UNTOUCHABLE LOVE
IS LIKE THE PULSE BENEATH MY SKIN,

THE RHYTHM OF MY DAYS,
AND THE ECHO IN THE EMPTINESS

UNTOUCHABLE LOVE IS INFINITE,
A FORCE THAT BENDS ALL OF NATURE.
I AM YOUR BEGINNING,
I AM YOUR MIDDLE,
I AM YOUR END,
THE WHOLE,
THE FIRE THAT BURNS ETERNALLY.

I KISS YOU IN THE NIGHT
I KISS YOU IN THE DAY
I KISS YOU IN THE STREET
I KISS YOU IN EVERY WAY
MY LOVE IS UNTOUCHABLE.

I AM DESIRE!

THE UNTOUCHABLE LOVE
A FORCE SO STRONG THE WORLD
DISSOLVES
TIME AND SPACE COLLIDE.

A LOVE WHERE ALL THE STARS RESIDE
A LOVE SO VAST
SO FREE
IT'S MIND-BLOWING

AN ENDLESS COSMIC SYMPHONY, THE
UNTOUCHABLE LOVE

THE GREAT CREATION WOMAN

IN THE BEGINNING,

GOD CREATED THE HEAVENS AND THE
EARTH,

BUT HIS GREATEST CREATION WAS
WOMAN HE BIRTHED

THE FIRST WOMAN EVE,

THE LADY OF THE GARDEN,

THE MOTHER OF ALL,

FROM THE GARDEN SHE HEARD THE
CALL,

WITH GRACE IN HER STEP AND
STRENGTH IN HER GAZE,

A FLAME IN HER SPIRIT, FOREVER A
BLAZE

GOD NEVER STOPPED DOING WONDERS,

ASK SARAH SHE KNOWS,

BLESSED IN HER TWILIGHT YEARS,

LAUGHTER AND HOPE WITH HER FAITH,

SHE CONQUERED ALL HER FEARS

WOMAN WAS FASHIONED NOT LAST BUT
GREATER,

WITH THE SPARK OF THE STARS AND A
BEACON OF STRENGTH,

DEBORAH, A WARRIOR, PROPHET, AND
JUDGE SO WISE,

A LEADER, A PRINCESS WHO HAD FIRE
IN HER EYES

SHE GUIDED MEN THROUGH BATTLE
AND STRIFE,

SHE WAS ONE TO RECKON WITH,

A COMMANDER OF LIFE.

SHE WAS MORE THAN A HELPER, MORE
THAN A PART,

SHE WAS WISDOM AND COURAGEOUS.
SHE WAS THE BEAT OF THE HEART

ESTHER,

THE QUEEN WHO DARED TO STAND,

SAVED HER PEOPLE AND CHALLENGED
TO SAVE THE LAND

THE BALANCE OF NATURE,

THE BREATH TO YOUR SOUL,

THIS BLACK WOMAN,

THE CREATOR MADE LIFE IN HER FULL
AND WHOLE.

RUTH, THIS BEAUTIFUL MOABITE BRIDE,

HER FAITH IN NAOMI, HER HEART
OPENED WIDE.

THROUGH LOVE AND LEGACY, SHE
BIRTHED A PRODIGY

WOMAN, HER HAIR LIKE RIVER,

HER VOICE IS LIKE THE WIND,

HER LAUGHTER LIKE RAIN WHEN THE
EARTH HAS SINNED.

MARY,

A PURE VESSEL CHOSEN FROM ABOVE,

THE MOTHER OF JESUS, A SYMBOL OF
LOVE

NOT FROM THE DUST LIKE THE
CREATURES AROUND,

BUT FROM LIVING FLESH,

WHERE LIFE WAS FIRST FOUND

GOMER,

THE HARLOT WHO STRAYED FAR AND WIDE,

LOVE PULLED HER BACK,

BUT THE WORLD CAST HER ASIDE.

A STORY OF GRACE THAT NEVER WOULD QUIT,

FORGIVENESS, AND MERCY WHERE SHADOWS SPLIT.

RAHAB THE WHORE,

HER NAME ETCHED IN FAME,

HER FAITH DEFIED ALL DOUBTS AND SHAME

WOMAN ROSE FROM THE RIB BY HIS DIVINE HAND,

A PARTNER, A DREAMER TO WALK GOD'S GREAT LAND

ABIGAIL,

WISE WITH A MIND THAT COULD SEE

ESCAPED THE ABUSE OF MAN AND
BECAME FREE

A VIRTUOUS WOMAN WHO CAN FIND,

BATHSHEBA

BATHED WHERE THE KING'S EYES DID
ROAM,

HER BEAUTY ENSNARED HIM AND
TARNISHED THE KING'S THRONE

WOMAN,

HER HANDS CRAFTED TO NURTURE AND
HEAL

A VESSEL OF MERCY OF TRUTH TO
REVEAL

FOR IN HER DESIGN,

A MIRACLE LAY,

THE ESSENCE OF LIFE IN A MORTAL
DISPLAY

DELILAH,

THE DECEIVER WITH BEAUTY SO KEEN,

HER WORDS WERE A WEAPON,

HER LIPS SHARP AND MEAN,

A TALE OF SEDUCTION THAT TURNED
LOVE INTO CLAY,

SHE CUT DOWN THE STRONGEST MAN
AND LED HIM ASTRAY

WOMAN,

ADAM AWOKE TO THIS VISION SO
BRIGHT,

A BEING OF WONDER, HIS HEART'S TRUE
DELIGHT.

BONE OF MY BONE,

HE WHISPERED IN AWE

FLESH OF MY FLESH,

THE FIRST LOVE HE SAW

MICHELLE THE POET

WHOSE WORDS SOAR HIGH ABOVE

CAPTURES THE TALES OF COURAGE
AND LOVE

WOMAN WAS FASHIONED,

NOT LAST BUT AS MORE,

A CROWN OF CREATION,

FOREVER ADORED

THE GREAT CREATION - WOMAN

JER 31:3

THE LORD HAS APPEARED OF OLD
TO ME

SAYING, YES, I HAVE LOVED YOU
WITH AN

EVERLASTING LOVE

THEREFORE, WITH
LOVINGKINDNESS

I HAVE DRAWN YOU

INTERLUDE 6

Dr. Michelle Stevens-O

Is the very embodiment of **resilience wrapped in grace**, a woman whose presence commands both reverence and warmth. When she enters a room, you don't just notice her, you **feel** her. Her strength is not loud or boastful; it's steady, rooted in years of pressing forward through life's storms. Every step she takes echoes with **faith, endurance, and quiet victory**.

She carries the essence of battles fought and won, not by chance, but by **unyielding trust in God**. Her life reflects perseverance born of purpose, and her walk is marked by both power and peace. To be in her presence is to feel **the stillness after chaos**, a sacred calm that reaches the soul. That peace doesn't come from circumstance; it comes from her deep intimacy with God and the certainty that His hand guides every part of her journey.

Walking beside her feels like walking in **triumph**. Each stride speaks of **overcoming odds**, of fear transformed into courage, of burdens lifted through belief. Her voice carries wisdom, measured, intentional, filled with truth and an anointing. She doesn't just speak **words**; she speaks **life**.

She is a vessel overflowing with divine fire, **untethered by expectation and unafraid of expansion**. God has entrusted her with vision, strength, and a mantle of leadership, and she wears it boldly. Dr. Michelle Stevens-O stands as a living testament that to walk in purpose is to walk in freedom, and to walk in freedom is to **walk boldly into the vastness of God's calling, unapologetic, unwavering, and unafraid.**

Love you Sisa

Gemetrious Carter

SHE IS BEAUTY

SHE IS THE REFLECTION OF SUN- KISSED
GLORY, WRAPPED IN MELANIN AND
MAGNIFICENT

BEAUTY THAT SPEAKS WITHOUT
WORDS AND RADIATES FROM THE
SOUL!

SHERO

GOD CALLS THE ORDINARY TO DO THE
EXTRAORDINARY,
MY SHERO IS EXEMPLARY

SHE CARRIES THE LINES ETCHED DEEP
IN HER FACE,
THAT SHOWS THE SACRIFICES WITH A
SILENT GRACE.

HER HANDS HAVE BUILT BRIDGES
WHERE NONE COULD STAND,
SHE HAS THE FORCE TO PUSH THROUGH
MOUNTAINS
AND THE STRENGTH OF THE
STRONGEST MAN

THERE ARE COUNTLESS NIGHTS SHE
STAYED AND PRAYED,
DETERMINED NONE WOULD GO ASTRAY

BATMAN NOT NEEDED
AND ROBIN WON'T DO,
SHE NEVER FALTERS,
SHE NEVER BREAKS,
SHE GIVES AND GIVES FOR OTHER'S
SAKE

SACRIFICE IS HER MIDDLE NAME,
WHEN I'M IN NEED SHE COMES TO LIFE
DOESN'T GIVE A SECOND THOUGHT,
AND DOESN'T THINK TWICE.

SHE MAKES A DOLLAR OUT OF A DIME,
EVEN WHEN SHE'S RUNNING OUT OF
TIME.
SHE MAKES A FEAST FROM AN EMPTY
SHELF,
ALWAYS PUTTING OTHERS BEFORE
HERSELF

SHE MAKES A MEAL OUT OF MAGIC,
EVEN WHEN SHE'S NOT FEELING WELL,
SHE PUSHES HERSELF AND OTHERS
CANNOT TELL

MY SHERO A SUPER WOMAN,
NO CAPE IS NEEDED AND CATWOMAN
CAN'T DO,
WHAT MY SHERO HAS HELPED ME
THROUGH

SHE PICKS ME UP WHEN I'M DOWN,
MY SHERO DON'T COME TO PLAY
GAMES
SHE COMES TO DO BUSINESS,

SHE DOESN'T MESS AROUND

HER LOVE IS A FIRE,
A FLAME SO STRONG,
THAT IT WARMS THE COLD,
A STORY OF COURAGE THAT'S NEVER
BEEN TOLD

SHE'S THE QUIET HERO WHO NEVER
ASKS,
THE ONE WHO COMPLETES IMPOSSIBLE
TASKS,
SHE CARRIES BURDENS THAT AREN'T
HER OWN,
THE WEIGHT OF THE WORLD SHE BEARS
ALONE

SHE'S THE LAUGHTER I LOOK FOR
AFTER A DAY OF TEARS,
THE COURAGE SHE GIVES THAT QUIETS
MY DEEPEST FEARS

SHE'S A DREAMER, A DOER,
A HEART SO BOLD
A LIVING LEGEND,
HER STORY YET TO BE TOLD,

SHE MAKES A WAY WHERE PATHS ARE
THIN,

TURNING EVERY LOSS INTO A WIN

HER SPIRIT IS FIERCE,
HER HEART SO WIDE,
A TRUE SHERO,
YOU CAN SEE THAT GOD ABIDES

A MOTHER, A SISTER, A FRIEND SO TRUE,
THE WORLD IS MUCH BRIGHTER
BECAUSE OF YOU

YOUR LEGACY IS LOVE, YOUR SPIRIT IS
FREE,
MY UNSUNG SHERO,
MEANS THE WORLD TO ME

SHE IS MY SHERO A FORCE UNTAMED
A WARRIOR SPIRIT, A SOUL UNCHAINED

SHE MAKES A WAY OUT OF NO WAY
NONE AT ALL,
LIFTING OTHERS UP SO THEY NEVER
FALL
SHERO

THE BEAUTY OF MIDNIGHT

I AM YOUR KNIGHT AND SHINING
ARMOR,

YOU ARE A BEAUTY SO PROFOUND,

SO DEEP, THAT ONLY MIDNIGHT DARES
TO KEEP

I AM THE PLACE WHERE SOULS REST,

IN MY SOLEMN CARE,

IN MY MIDNIGHTS COOL AIR.

I AM THE PLACE WHERE SHADOWS
DANCE,

IN THE GENTLE STARS LIGHT,

WHERE THE MOON GIVES ITS SOFT
GLOW AND SHINES ACROSS THE SKY SO
BRIGHT.

COME RUN WITH ME AS MIDNIGHTS
MAGIC STARTS TO UNFOLD,

AND WHERE TRUE LOVE STORIES ARE
TOLD

LET ME HOLD YOU CLOSE IN THE HUSH
OF MIDNIGHTS DEEP EMBRACE,

WHEN THE WORLD IS STILL,

AND TIME SLOWS ITS PACE

I GUARD YOUR DREAMS,

YOUR HEART AND I CALM YOUR MIND,

IN ME YOUR TRUEST PEACE YOU FIND.

I AM MIDNIGHT,

I LOVE WITHOUT A SINGLE WORD,

MY VOICE IS THE NIGHTS WIND SOFTLY
HEARD.

IN MIDNIGHTS LOVE THERE'S NO RUSH
AND NO DEMAND,

ONLY ME EXTENDING MY LOVING HAND

RUN, RUN WITH ME THROUGH THIS
STARY NIGHT,

BEFORE MIDNIGHT FADES AND WE
BEGIN TO KISS THE MORNING LIGHT

I AM MIDNIGHT,

MY WHISPERS CRADLE ALL WHO SEEK,

I HAVE A LOVE SO STRONG YET CALM
AND MEEK

MIDNIGHT, THE WORLD IS HUSHED
BENEATH MY GAZES

AS STARS DANCE AND IGNITE IN ITS
QUIET PRAISE

I AM THE BEAUTY OF MIDNIGHT

BLACK GIRL MAGIC

AT BIRTH, MAGIC TOOK A NEW FORM,
A MELODY OF GRACE,
AND POWER WAS BORN

BLACK GIRL MAGIC!

MY SKIN IS KISSED BY THE SUN'S
EMBRACE,
RAYS OF FABULOUS HUES ONLY TIME
CAN TRACE.

THERE IS STRENGTH IN MY HAIR,
IN EVERY LOCK AND EVERY CURL,
WHERE GALAXIES ARE PINNED,
A UNIVERSE OF POWER VIBRANT
WITHIN.

MY VOICE CAN BE LOUD,
SOFT AND STRONG,
MY LAUGHTER IS LIKE THUNDER,
EARTH SHAKING AND FREE,
AN ECHO YOU HEAR OF MY ANCESTORS'
LEGACY

I AM MAGIC, NO CHAINS CAN BIND ME,
AND NO WORDS CAN DEFINE ME.

I AM BLACK GIRL MAGIC,
BOLD AND TRUE,
YOU SEE MY MAGIC IN EVERYTHING I
DO.

WITH ONE TOUCH IT CHANGES,
IT TRANSFORMS.
IT'S NOT DONE BY SUCH LUCK,
NOPE, IT'S BLACK GIRL MAGIC
WITH A GRACEFUL TOUCH

THERE'S MAGIC IN EVERY STEP I TAKE,
I AM THE TRUTH.

YOU STOP AND TAKE NOTICE AS I WALK
BY.
I'M MORE THAN YOU SEE,
I'M A BLEND OF MY ANCESTORS' ROOTS
AND HISTORY.

YOU SEE COURAGE IN MY STRIDE,
A QUIET STRENGTH, I DO NOT HIDE.

I AM THE STORM,
THE CALM AND THE FLAME
A FORCE THAT NO ONE DARES TO TAME.

MY MAGIC WILL MAKE YOU BELIEVE,

YOU CAN CLIMB THE HIGHEST
MOUNTAIN AND SWIM THE DEEPEST
SEA.
THE MAGIC IN ME, MAKES YOU BELIEVE
IN YOU.

IT'S BLACK GIRL MAGIC
GOD IS WITHIN ME, I WILL NOT FAIL
I'M A WARRIOR, A POET, A QUEEN SO
DIVINE,
I AM BLACK GIRL MAGIC, YES, I'M ONE
OF A KIND

BLACK GIRL MAGIC!

SHE IS LOVE

HER LOVE IS LEGACY, SOFT
ENOUGH TO HEAL, STRONG
ENOUGH TO BUILD,

 AND DEEP ENOUGH TO CARRY
GENERATIONS FORWARD

AARON'S ROD

IN THE BEGINNING, GOD CREATED THE
HEAVENS AND THE EARTH,

THEN HE STOOD BACK AND TOOK A
LOOK

HE SAID IT ALL LOOKS GOOD, AND DEEP
IN THOUGHT, HE SHOOK HIS HEAD IN A
NOD,

HE SAID I NEED TO BRING JOY TO THE
WORLD, THEN HE CREATED AARON'S
ROD

WITH THE STRIKE OF LIGHTNING, AND
THE SOUND OF THUNDER,

A MASTER'S PIECE, EXOTIC, EROTIC,
GEOMETRIC, DYNAMIC CREATION,

THAT FULFILLS THE GREATEST FANTASY
OF EVERY NATION

IT HAS VIGOR, IT HAS POWER,

THE CURVE OF THIS ROD, NO ONE CAN DEVOUR

WITH ONE TOUCH, IT IGNITES A SPARK,

CREATING AN ELECTRIC FIRE,

IT AWAKENS A BURNING THAT YIELDS A DEEP DESIRE

THE ACHE OF LOVE, SUCH YEARNING IT CAUSES,

BUILT STURDY AND SOME ARE BUILT WIDE,

AARONS ROD AT ATTENTION YOU CANNOT HIDE

IT RISES, IT FALLS, LIKE A SNAKE IT SWAYS,

SOFT HANDS EXPLORE IT, WITH GENTLE LIPS IN PLEASURE IT GIVES WAY TO THE PLAY

AARONS ROD, LONG AND STRONG,

HAS WOMEN CONSUMED BY PASSION AND SINGING A BRAND-NEW SONG

IT CREATES A CRAVING THAT DRIVES
WOMEN WILD,

A FUSION OF POWER, TENDER,

IT TAMES THE WILDEST WOMAN AND
MAKES HER MILD

SOME WOMEN FIGHT AND SOME ARE ON
EDGE,

WITH TIME SUSPEND, IN ITS EMBRACE,

IN MOMENTS, YOU WILL GIVE TO ITS
BEND

WITH A TOUCH AND A GENTLE WIND
BREEZE,

IT COMES TO LIFE, WITH A TENDER EASE

IT GIVES, NOT JUST A FLEETING THRILL,

BUT A PASSION, A LONGING, A DESIRE SO
REAL

THE MIND DISSOLVES, THE SENSES
REIGN,

WE GRASP THE WORLD OF PLEASURE
FACE TO FACE, WE FEEL NO SHAME

HER BODY OPENS WIDE AND FREE,

SHE YIELDS TO AARON'S ROD,

AS IT ENTERS THE VESSEL OF ETERNITY,

AND SHE TASTES THE DEPTHS OF
ECSTASY

NO WORDS ARE NEEDED,

NO PROMISES MADE,

ONCE YOU GET A HOLD OF AARONS
ROD,

YOU BECOME ITS SLAVE, AARONS ROD

COURAGE

WHO AM I, I AM COURAGE
COURAGE IS THE BEAUTY OF A SOUL
LAID BARE.
I CATCH YOU IN THE WIND,
I AM THE BREEZE YOU FEEL ACROSS
YOUR SKIN.

WHO AM I, I AM COURAGE

I AM FOUND IN MOMENTS WHERE
OTHERS RETREAT,
IN THE STEADY PULSE,
THE UNWAVERING BEAT.

WHO AM I, I AM COURAGE

I AM, THE BRAVE YOU NEED,
IN EVERY ACT OF COURAGE,
THERE'S A GRACE, A BEAUTY, THAT
TIME CAN NEVER ERASE

WHO AM I, I AM COURAGE

THE LIGHT IN THE DARKEST HOUR,
A FORCE SO STRONG,
IN A VOICE THAT QUIVERS,

YET SPEAKS WITHOUT DOUBT.

WHO AM I, I AM COURAGE

I WILL PUSH YOU THROUGH YOUR
DOUBTS AND YOUR FEARS,
I HOLD YOU CLOSE, SO TIGHT, SO DEAR.

WHO AM I, I AM COURAGE

I AM, LIKE THE LOVE OF A STRONG
EMBRACE,
THAT WHISPERS IN THE QUIET,
THE UNSEEN, THE UNHEARD.
COURAGE IS LIKE A LOVE THAT MOVES
WITHOUT A WORD.

WHO AM I, I AM COURAGE

I AM, FOUND IN THE MOMENT YOU
CHOOSE TO BE BRAVE,
IN THE FACE OF THE STORM, IN THE
STRENGTH YOU CRAVE

WHO AM I, I AM COURAGE

HOLD YOUR HEAD HIGH,
GREET THE WORLD WITH A SMILE.

I AM COURAGE, BEAUTY IN ITS PUREST
FORM.

WHO AM I, I AM COURAGE

THROUGH EVERY TRIAL AND EVERY
PAIN,
I HOLD STEADY, I REMAIN, TRUE!
I AM, LIKE THE BREAKING OF DAWN,
THE LIGHT THAT SHINES THROUGH

WHO AM I, I AM COURAGE

I AM THE ROCK THAT STRENGTHENS
YOUR HANDS FOR WAR AND YOUR
FINGERS FOR THE FIGHT.
I AM A FLAME THAT NEVER BURN OUT.

WHO AM I, I AM, THE REINFORCEMENT
YOU NEED,
I AM COURAGE

TRUTHFULLY

LOVE IS PATIENT
LOVE IS KIND
I GET A CHILL AND A THRILL
IN DISCOVERING A LOVE SO REAL

I WILL CLIMB THE HIGHEST MOUNTAIN
I WILL SWIM THE DEEPEST SEA
FOR YOUR LOVE IS LIKE HOT LAVA
THAT MELTS ALL OVER ME

IN YOUR PRESENCE
THE WORLD FEELS WHOLE
YOU ARE THE KEEPER OF MY SOUL

I HAVE SEARCHED HIGH AND LOW
YOUR LOVE IS SO GOOD YOU DESERVE
ENCORE
A STANDING OVATION IS GIVEN TO YOU

YOU HAVE HIT A HIGH SCORE, MY ME
AMOUR

TRUTHFULLY

AS I EXPLORE THIS THING CALLED
LOVE

IT'S A DIVINE PURSUIT

TRANSCENDING ALL OF TIME

ONCE I START

YOU WILL NEVER WANT TO PART

YOUR LAUGHTER IS LIKE THE MORNING
SUN

WHEN I THINK ABOUT THE WAY YOU
HOLD ME AND TOUCH ME

ALL I WANT IS ANOTHER MOMENT WITH
YOU

TO ALLOW IT TO BE

TO LOVE THIS WAY

IS TO LOSE CONTROL

I CHOOSE YOU TO BE ALL UP IN ME

ALLOWING ALL OF CREATION TO
EXPLODE INSIDE OF ME

YOU STOLE MY HEART AWAY

I CAN NOT LET YOU ESCAPE

SO TAKE MY LOVE

OR LET IT BE

BUT KNOW IT FLOWS ETERNALLY

YOUR LOVE TURNS ME INSIDE OUT

MAKING ME LAUGH

MAKING ME CRY

WITH EVERY STROKE I GIVE A LOUD
SOOTHING SIGH

WE HAVE AN ESSENCE OF ECSTASY

NOT JUST A FLUTTER OF THE HEART

YOU TAKE COMMAND OF EVERY PART

IT REACHES HIGH

IT DIVIDES BELOW

ONLY TO PLACES YOU ARE ALLOWED TO
GO

TRUTHFULLY

THIS LOVE HAS A FORCE THAT REFINES
ME

REMOVING ALL FLAWS

ALL FEARS

THAT ONCE DEFINED ME

THIS LOVE FILLS EVERY VOID IN MY
HEART

IT MOLDS US TOGETHER

DOWN TO THE DEEPEST PART

TO LOVE THIS DEEP

IS NOT SO LIGHT

UNDERSTANDING, INSPIRING

IT MAKES YOU FEEL

FABULOUS AND DANGEROUS TOO

IT HAS YOU FLOATING THROUGH THE
DAY AND NIGHT

TRUTHFULLY

EVEN IF IT LEAVES ME TORN

THE DEPTH OF THIS LOVE IS WHY I WAS
BORN

THROUGH STORMS AND TRAILS

HIGHS AND LOWS

IT'S WITH YOU A DEVOTION GROWS

IT BENDS, IT BREAKS

IT MENDS, IT HEALS

LOVE IS ALL I AM

IT'S ALL I FEEL

I SEE THE STRENGTH IN YOUR EYES

A QUIET FIRE, A DEEP DESIRE THAT
NEVER DIES

IN YOUR LOVE I HAVE A SACRED PLACE

PROTECTED I FEEL IN YOUR WARM
EMBRACE

NO OCEAN'S DEPTH

NO STAR-FILLED SKY

CAN MATCH THIS LOVE I HOLD INSIDE

THIS HOLD YOU HAVE ON ME, HAS
ROOTED ITSELF, UNYIELDING AND
PURE, HAS BUILT A BOND TIME CAN NOT
OBSCURE

WITH EVERY BREATH, I BREATHE

I SAY OH WOW

I LOVE YOU MORE THAN I THOUGHT I
KNEW HOW

HERE I STAND FOREVER TRUE

MY DEEPEST LOVE BELONGS TO YOU

TRUTHFULLY

PSALM 17:8

KEEP ME AS THE APPLE OF YOUR EYE

**HIDE ME UNDER THE SHADOW OF
YOUR WINGS**

INTERLUDE 7

Many are called, but few are chosen, and you, my sister, are among the chosen. You have risen with grace, endured with strength, and now stand fully poised to take your rightful place upon the royal throne as Queen.

Dr. Stevens-O, I vividly recall our very first, spirit-filled encounter. Though I wasn't certain when or how our paths would cross again, I always knew they would. And now, I give thanks to God for satisfying that quiet longing, for divinely repositioning you in this season, so that you might continue to illuminate the path for other women, me included.

We both know that nothing happens by chance. God doesn't deal in coincidences; He works in purpose. Our connection holds deeper meaning, and I believe it is the beginning of something greater, something impactful, far beyond what we can yet imagine.

For now, continue to walk boldly. **Go pave the way. Do what Queens do.** Lead with purpose, walk in power, and never forget that your presence is both prophetic and necessary.

Know this—I carry your wisdom with me. Your words have planted seeds, and I will water them as I rise to new levels. And know this, too—this divine appointment was not the end, but the beginning. We have a mission to fulfill—and together, **we will be victorious.**

In Black Excellence & Divine Purpose,

Dr. Catinia Farrington

STRENGTH OF A BLACK WOMAN

SHE BENDS BUT NEVER BREAKS,
RISING WITH GRACE THROUGH
STORMS MEANT TO

SILENCE HER, BECAUSE HER
STRENGTH WAS NEVER BORN
FROM EASE, BUT WITH PURPOSE

BEAUTY IN BLACK

BEAUTY AND GREATNESS RISE FROM
THE DARKEST PLACES,
HAVE YOU SEEN ME,
THEY CALL ME BLACK
I AM THE BEAUTY OF THE MOABITE
BLACK

THIS BEAUTY IS ONLY FOUND IN THE
UNEXPECTED,
THE MOST BEAUTIFUL ESSENCE OF
COLOR YOU'VE NEVER SEEN

FROM THE DARKEST ONYX TO COCOA'S
HUE,
THE MASTER'S VANILLA BEST FLAVOR,
AND CARAMEL COLORS TOO,
I AM A MASTER'S PIECE

I AM BEAUTY, I AM POISED, GRACEFUL,
AND QUALIFIED,
I DON'T NEED YOUR PERMISSION TO
EXIST, I AM!

A QUEEN, IN STRENGTH AND GRACE
PROFOUND

I AM DEVALUED, DISMISSED, DENIED,
AND DEEMED DANGEROUS,
I AM EXCEPTIONAL,
YES EXCEPTIONALLY BLACK,
THAT'S ME, I AM THE EXCEPTION

I CANNOT BE SILENCED,
WHEN I AM FULLY SEEN IN ALL MY
BLACKNESS,
IN MY PAIN, AND IN MY POWER,
THE BLACK BEAUTY COMES WITH A
PURPOSE, TO DEVOUR

THIS BLACK IS OVERLOOKED,
DISMISSED, AND EVEN DEGRADED,
I'M NOTHING AND EVERYTHING AT THE
SAME TIME,
BUT THE BEAUTY OF MY BLACKNESS IS
LIKE GOD,
I CONTROL ALL OF THE UNIVERSE AND
ALL OF TIME

I CARRY THE WEIGHT OF EVERY BLACK
SISTAH,
BIG, TALL, SHORT AND SMALL,

THROUGH STORMS I'VE WALKED,
THROUGH TRIALS VAST,
MY POWER ETCHED ALONG LIFE PATHS

THE LIGHT I CARRY, AND THE SCARS I
OWN
THIS BLACK YIELDS A TOUCH WITH
POWER AND STRONG,
SOFT AS A WHISPER, BEHELD LIKE A
LOVE SONG

THIS BLACK BEAUTY,
UNTOUCHABLE, TIMELESS, FIERCE AND
WHOLE
A TESTAMENT TO AN UNBREAKABLE
SOUL

WITH MY ARMOR STRONG,
I STAND SUPREME,
YOU TAKE AWE AT THE BEAUTY OF THIS
BLACK QUEEN

THE EARTH WAS SHAPED IN
BLACKENED STONE,
MY MIGHT UNMATCH, MY STRENGTH
UNKNOWN,
MY SKIN A PIECE OF TAPESTRY,
EACH SHADE DRAWN WITH COLORS OF
FINE ARTISTRY

THEY STAND AT AWE, THIS BLACK TO BE
ADORED,

IN HISTORY'S STORYBOOKS,
NO ONE CAN REWRITE THIS SCORE

SO, HONOR THIS BLACK BEAUTY,
IT'S POWERFUL AND RARE,
THIS COLOR SO RICH,
IT'S FIERCE AND GRACEFUL BEYOND
COMPARE

BEAUTY IN BLACK

BLACK GIRL RISE

WITH HAIR SO KINKY, THE WORLD ONCE
TOLD HER SHE COULDN'T BE,

THAT DREAMS LIKE HERS WEREN'T
MEANT TO BREATHE

IN HER HEART A FIRE BURNED SO
BRIGHT

SHE TURNED THEIR NO'S INTO HER
FIGHT

FROM ROOTS THAT RUN THROUGH
SACRED GROUND

A QUEEN IS BORN, HER STRENGTH
PROFOUND

THROUGH STORMS SHE WALKS

THROUGH FIRE SHE'S RUN

NO CHAIN COULD HOLD HER

NO WALL COULD CONTAIN HER

SHE CAME FROM STREETS WHERE
DREAMS WERE FRAIL

WHERE HOPES WERE LOST, A FRAGILE TALE

THE CORNERS TAUGHT HER GRIT AND GRACE

SURVIVAL ETCHED UPON HER FACE

IN HER HEART, A VISION GREW

OF WORLDS BEYOND THE ONE SHE KNEW

THROUGH CRACKED CONCRETE,

A PLACE WITH POTHOLES IN THE STREET

SHE FOUND HER BLOOM

DEFYING THE ODDS, SHE ESCAPED THE GLOOM

TO THE CORPORATE WORLD,
UNACCEPTABLE, DENIABLE, A DISTANT STAR

YET PRESSING FORWARD, A REACH THOUGHT TO BE TOO FAR

BLACK POWER SUIT, MARKS THE GRIND

HER FOOTPRINTS LEAD UP THE LADDER,
SHE DARED TO CLIMB

WITH EVERY STRIDE SHE CLAIMED HER
SPACE

A BLACK GIRL RISING WITH POISE AND
GRACE

HER VOICE WAS BOLD, MAKING HER
PRESENCE CLEAR

SHE SHATTERED HIGH CEILINGS THEY
HELD SO DEAR

STRUGGLES MET HER AT EVERY TURN

WARRING THROUGH THE BATTLE
WHERE STRENGTH IS EARNED

GLASS CEILINGS CRACKED BENEATH
HER STRIDE

IN EACH STEP A TRIUMPH, A SOURCE OF
PRIDE

HER VOICE A SONG, HER POWER DIVINE

SHE REWRITES HER FATE WITH EVERY
LINE

SHE WALKS WITH GRACE, HER HEAD
HELD HIGH

THE WORLD TAKES NOTICE, THEY STOP
AND STARE

THERE'S MAGIC IN THE WAY SHE MOVES

A STATEMENT IN HOW SHE STYLES HER
HAIR

A CASCADE OF COILS, WITH A DARING
FRAME

SHE'S A FORCE OF NATURE THEY CAN
NOT CONTAIN

LONGING ADMIRATION, BEARS A
MIGHTY STING

A GREAT JEALOUSY RISE AND ENVY IS
EVERYTHING

SOME CRAVE HER GLOW, OTHERS
WONDER HOW SHE SHINE

WITH BEWILDERMENT IN THEIR MIND

SHE IS MORE THAN LOOKS, SHE IS
CROWNED, ADORED, DIVINE,

A BLACK GIRL RISING, SHE IS ONE OF A
KIND

A BLACK WOMAN CROWNED IN EARNED
SUCCESS

SHE'S LIVING PROOF OF NOTHING LESS

TO RISE, TO CLAIM, TO NEVER BEND

A LEGACY SHE LEAVES, THAT WILL
NEVER END

SHE'S PROOF OF WHAT THE WORLD
CAN'T SEE

THAT GREATNESS THRIVES WHERE IT
SHOULDN'T BE

FROM THE GHETTO'S ROOTS TO THE
BOARDROOM HEIGHTS

A BLACK GIRL SHINE HER FUTURE
BRIGHT

SHE ROSE, SHE SOARED, SHE CLAIMED
HER PRIZE

A TESTAMENT TO HOW A BLACK GIRL
RISE

BLACK GIRL RISE

THE DETERMINATION OF A BLACK WOMAN

A BLACK WOMAN'S DETERMINATION IS DIVINE, ROOTED IN FAITH, FUELED BY

FIRE, AND DESTINED TO BREAK BARRIERS OTHERS DARE NOT APPROACH

DO NOT LET YOUR ADORNMENT BE
MERELY OUTWARD

ARRANGING THE HAIR, WEARING
GOLD

OR PUTTING ON FINE APPAREL,
RATHER

LET IT BE THE HIDDEN PERSON OF
THE HEART

WITH THE INCORRUPTIBLE BEAUTY

OF A GENTLE AND QUIET SPIRIT
WHICH IS VERY PRECIOUS IN THE
SIGHT OF GOD

DEAR GOD

DEAR GOD,

YOU FORMED ME AND FASHIONED ME

MADE ME INTO THE IMAGE YOU
DESIRED OF ME

YOU SEE ME WITH A GAZE SO DEEP AND
A LOVE SO KIND,

I HAVE BEEN CHOSEN,

I AM YOURS,

YOU CALLED ME THE APPLE OF YOUR
EYE

I AM AN HEIR,

A GREAT INHERITANCE I HAVE IN YOU,

YOU GIVE ME TREASURES OUT OF
DARKNESS

AND RICHES HIDDEN IN SECRET PLACES
A NEW

I AM REDEEMED, FORGIVEN, AND
WHOLE,

A PRECIOUS JEWEL A TREASURED SOUL

DEAR GOD

I AM CALLED BY YOUR NAME AND
WRAPPED IN YOUR FRAME

YOUR VOICE I KNOW,

A WHISPER BELOVED YOU BELONG TO
ME,

I AM HEALED BY YOUR STRIPES, I AM
FREE

YOU CALLED ME BLESSED,

YOUR CHERISHED BRIDE,

IN YOU I FIND MY STRENGTH,

MY JOY, MY PEACE, AND MY PRIDE

DEAR GOD

I THANK YOU FOR EVERY BREATH I
TAKE

IN THE MORNING WHEN I WAKE,

FOR LIGHT AND THE DAWN THAT
BREAKS

DEAR GOD

IN YOU THERE'S A LOVE THAT KNOWS
NO END,

YOU ARE MY FATHER AND MY CLOSEST
FRIEND

I AM A NEW CREATURE,

MY FOOTSTEPS ARE ORDERED FOR THE
PATH YOU'VE SET,

FOR EACH STEP I TAKE

WITH THE COURAGE TO RISE AFTER
EVERY MISTAKE

I AM THE RIGHTEOUSNESS OF GOD

DEAR GOD,

YOU CREATED THE SUN AND THE
GENTLE RAIN,

I HAVE FOUND JOY AND LAUGHTER IN
THE MIDST OF GREAT ENDURING PAIN.

FOR EVERY TEAR I CRIED,

THEY CLEANSED MY SOUL,

ALL MY BROKEN PIECES,

YOU GATHERED THEM UP AND MADE
ME WHOLE

DEAR GOD,

THANK YOU FOR EVERY DREAM YOU
MADE NEW,

YOU REDEEMED ME FROM THE ENEMY

AND GIVEN ME FAITH THAT GROWS AS I
LEAN ON YOU

DEAR GOD,

YOU SAY I AM YOUR GLORY,

YOU HAVE GIVEN ME GRACE I DON'T
DESERVE,

YOU HAVE GIVEN ME MERCY
UNEARNED,

AND YOUR LOVE UNRESERVED

I AM YOUR RIGHTEOUSNESS,

YOU CALLED ME YOUR CHILD,

YOUR OWN,

YOU TELL ME I HAVE A MANSION I CAN
CALL HOME.

I AM A ROYAL PRIESTHOOD SET APART,

CARVED WITH LOVE,

AND WRITTEN ON THE TABLET OF YOUR
HEART.

DEAR GOD,

THIS POEM I WRITE JUST FOR YOU,

I THANK YOU FOR EVERY PROMISE AND
EVERY TRUTH

I AM WHO YOU SAY I AM

I WALK BY FAITH,

HELD IN YOUR LOVE WRAPPED IN YOUR
GRACE

THANK YOU FOR THE GIFT OF LIFE

AND THE GIFT OF YOUR SON,

FOR EVERY MOMENT BIG AND SMALL,

THANK YOU FOR BEING MY GOD,

THE GIVER OF ALL

DEAR GOD

Ecclesiastes 3:11

HE HAS MADE EVERYTHING
BEAUTIFUL IN ITS TIME

Back Cover Description for *Beauty of the Black Swan*

Beauty of the Black Swan is a breathtaking collection of poetry inspired by the grace and wisdom of God. Each verse is a celebration of resilience, strength, and the unique beauty that resides within every Black woman. From moments of healing to bursts of laughter, from quiet reflection to the unshakable pride of heritage, this book offers something for every woman to hold close to her heart.

With themes of faith, self-discovery, and empowerment woven through its pages, *Beauty of the Black Swan* is more than a book; it's a journey. Whether you are mending wounds, seeking inspiration, or embracing the powerful woman you were always meant to be, this collection will speak to your soul.

For every woman who has ever felt unseen or underestimated, *Beauty of the Black Swan* is a radiant reminder of your worth, your purpose, and your God-given beauty. This is poetry to heal, to uplift,

and to make you proud of the incredible
woman you are.

Dr. Michelle Stevens-Oldham is a Black female author, minister, speaker, and transformation coach who has dedicated her life to helping women heal, rise, and walk boldly in their God-given purpose. As a woman who has experienced profound loss, hardship, incarceration, and homelessness, her story is one of radical redemption and unwavering faith. Through every trial, she discovered not just survival, but rebirth.

Dr. Stevens-Oldham is the visionary founder of **Direction at Midlife**, a coaching and empowerment platform created to guide women in their 40s, 50s, and beyond through emotional healing, mindset renewal, and personal transformation. Her mission is to reach those who feel forgotten, broken, or uncertain, and remind them that they are still powerful, still chosen, and still destined for greatness.

With a background in ministry, leadership, and business, Dr. Stevens-

Oldham combines spiritual insight with practical tools to lead women into wholeness. She is also the host of the podcast *"Direction at Midlife,"* where she shares transparent conversations about faith, trauma, healing, and rebuilding life after personal storms.

Beauty of the Black Swan is her poetic offering to women of color, a celebration of identity, divine strength, and the sensual, sacred complexity of Black womanhood. Her words pour from a place of deep healing, calling others to embrace both their beauty and their brokenness as holy ground.

Dr. Stevens-Oldham currently resides in South Carolina with her husband and family, where she continues to write, teach, and inspire.